FROM STRESS TO REST

Benjamin Smith, Sr.

FROM STRESS TO REST

Copyright © 1998 by Benjamin Smith, Sr.

All rights reserved. No part of this publication may be reproduced, stored in a retrieval system, or transmitted in any form or by means electronic, mechanical, photocopying, recording, or otherwise, except for the inclusion of brief quotations in a review, without prior permission in writing from the publishers.

Scriptures taken from the
HOLY BIBLE, King James Version.

ISBN 0-939241-35-8

Published by
Deliverance Evangelistic Church
2001 W. Lehigh Avenue
Philadelphia, PA 19132
(215) 226-7600

Printed in the United States of America.

CONTENTS

Introduction		5
Chapter 1	THE DIVINE INVITATION	7
Chapter 2	THE GREAT STRUGGLE	14
Chapter 3	"WHERE CAN I FIND PEACE?"	22
Chapter 4	AN AWESOME TRANSFORMATION	28
Chapter 5	DON'T SETTLE FOR SUBSTITUTES	37
Chapter 6	REST IN THE SPIRIT	44
Chapter 7	THE FAITH FACTOR	51
Chapter 8	WHO CAN YOU TRUST?	58
Chapter 9	CONNECTED TO THE SOURCE	65
Chapter 10	"LEARN OF ME"	73
Chapter 11	YOU'RE BEING PERFECTED!	80
Chapter 12	TOTAL REST	88

INTRODUCTION

If the first few minutes of the nightly news is any indication, this world is in deep trouble. The newscaster gives the headlines: "Rebel troops are about to enter a foreign capital." "A serial killer is on the loose in one of America's major cities." "A politician is being indicted for unethical conduct."

Those are just the national stories. If you turned the camera around and focused on the life of each viewer, you would find a similar scenario — a life under siege and a soul under stress.

As a pastor, the message of this book has weighed heavily on my heart. I have counseled with far too many people who do not fully realize that the Prince of Peace has a plan to bring rest to all who will ask.

Make no mistake; Satan is still prowling the earth bringing fear to hearts and anguish to the minds of those who heed his evil thoughts.

I have written this message so that you can escape the

clutches of the Evil One and find the abundant life that only Christ can offer.

In these pages you will learn:

- How to find God's peace and tranquility.
- The secret of winning the battle between the flesh and the Spirit.
- Keys to discovering internal security.
- Where to find hidden strength.
- How to avoid Satan's substitutes.
- How to communicate with the Comforter.
- The power of mixing the message with faith.
- How to regain trust and confidence.
- How to stay connected to heaven.
- Lessons from the Great Teacher.
- Principles of being perfected.
- How to find eternal rest.

I earnestly pray that as you digest these pages and apply God's Word, you will embark on the greatest adventure of your life — the journey from stress to rest.

1

THE DIVINE INVITATION

We are living in an age of anxiety. Everywhere I look people are disturbed by fears, doubts and apprehensions. They are deeply troubled by:

- The pressure of finances.
- Tension in their marriage.
- Conflicts with their children.
- Worry about their health.
- Turmoil in their workplace.
- Violence in their neighborhoods.

Tears were streaming down the face of a man who recently came to my office. He pulled his chair close to me and cried, "Pastor, I don't know what in the world to do. I am overwhelmed by circumstances and conditions that seem beyond my control."

Not only are the ungodly living under stress; I see it in the lives of far too many of God's children. They are existing needlessly in a state of uncertainty and confusion.

Here's something else I've discovered:

People attempt to apply human solutions to spiritual needs. It won't work!

There is an answer that can lift the burden you carry. It's a heavenly answer!

The Fatal Mistake

What is the basic cause of man's plight? We have to journey back to the beginning.

God created a beautiful, magnificent world. The Creator saw everything He had made, "And, behold, it was very good" (Genesis 1:31).

Then the Almighty created man and gave him dominion over His earthly kingdom. It was a place of perfection and harmony. Nothing was lacking.

God also gave man a commandment which served as a test. It came in the form of a warning that if he sinned it would bring death.

Adam and Eve did not listen. They ate of the tree that was forbidden and from that moment sin entered the heart of man. Then, when Adam died, Satan introduced death into the human family and to this day the devil attempts to control us.

The problem that continues to plague man originated with Satan — God's right-hand cherub. He was the master of the heavenly choir; the most beautiful of all creatures who became lifted up in pride.

Satan came to the conclusion that he didn't want to be equal with God, but that he should establish his throne *above* God.

Although the devil lost the battle with the Almighty, he has never stopped his relentless pursuit of man. As a result the human race faces an enormous obstacle on its road to deliverance.

Oh, What an Invitation!

The problem is immense. However, the solution is more than adequate. The answer is not found in religion, nor in an experience. It is found in a person — Jesus Christ.

God sent His only begotten Son to be born as a man, yet to die on a cross. His blood was shed at Calvary to cover our sin and cleanse us from all unrighteousness.

Jesus died and was buried. Thankfully, the story doesn't end there. On the third day He rose from the grave. Hallelujah! He ascended to heaven and right now — *at this very moment* — He sits at the right hand of God making intercession for you to the Heavenly Father.

FROM STRESS TO REST

Today, the Lord gives a call to all men and women who find themselves struggling against evil. It's a Divine invitation.

Jesus stretches out His arms to a weary world and says:

> *"Come unto me, all ye that labor and are heavy laden, and I will give you rest. Take my yoke upon you, and learn of me; for I am meek and lowly in heart: and ye shall find rest unto your souls. For my yoke is easy, and my burden is light."*
> *— Matthew 11:28-30*

This was not the first time the Divine invitation was extended. God announced it hundreds of years earlier when He spoke these glorious words through the prophet Isaiah: "Ho, every one that thirsteth, come ye to the waters, and he that hath no money; come ye, buy, and eat; yea, come, buy wine and milk without money and without price" (Isaiah 55:1).

He declared: "Wherefore do ye spend money for that which is not bread? And your labor for that which satisfieth not? Hearken diligently unto me, and eat ye that which is good, and let your soul delight itself in fatness. Incline your ear, and come unto me: hear, and your soul shall live; and I will make an everlasting covenant with you, even the sure mercies of David" (vv.2-3).

"Whosoever Will"

The Lord's invitation is not limited to a chosen few, but offered to *all*. Jesus says: "Whosoever will come after me, let him deny himself, and take up his cross, and follow me" (Mark 8:34).

This is not a proposal to better ourselves intellectually or socially. It is a call for a total regeneration — from the inside out.

Those with academic skills or political power may leave their mark on society. They may be remembered by having a bronze statue erected in the courtyard of City Hall. Their names may be inscribed in granite on great buildings. People may celebrate their birth and death. However, if these acclaimed men and women have not been resurrected from spiritual death, it is all for naught. The question is this: Where will you spend eternity?

It requires a personal response to the Lord's call to prepare us for the world to come.

The Bible is a supernatural document. It is not the product of man's mind; it was delivered by the Spirit of God. And the results of the Gospel are also beyond human explanation. "Therefore if any man be in Christ, he is a new creature: old things are passed away; behold, all things are become new" (2 Corinthians 5:17).

I would love to be able to tell you that the moment you give your heart to Christ every problem of your life will cease. I wish that were the case. The battle continues because "We wrestle not against flesh and blood, but against principalities, against powers, against the rulers of the darkness of this world, against spiritual wickedness in high places" (Ephesians 6:12).

When Jesus, the second Adam, descended from heaven and took on human flesh, Satan immediately tried to seduce him. But God gave Jesus power over the devil — and He desires to give us that same authority.

For those who have not accepted Christ, their father is still Satan. As Jesus declared to the religious leaders of His day, "Ye are of your father the devil, and the lusts of your father ye will do. He was a murderer from the beginning, and abode not in the truth, because there is no truth in him. When he speaketh a lie, he speaketh of his own: for he is a liar, and the father of it" (John 8:44).

Are You Ready?

Men scramble and claw their way to the highest peaks — politically, socially and intellectually — only to find that there are no more mountains to conquer. They become disillusioned and discouraged.

Perhaps you are weary of your attempts to escape from the valley — exhausted from traveling the long, lonesome road.

The Divine Invitation

The message you will find in this book was written to give you strength for your journey. I believe God can restore your vision, lift your burden and raise you to new heights. And I pray that you will be able to stand and declare, "My eyes have seen the glory of the Lord."

- Are you ready to be resurrected from spiritual death?
- Are you ready to let go of the world that is pulling you into darkness?
- Are you ready to find God's peace and tranquility?
- Are you ready to hear the heavenly call?

There is something about the voice of the Master that drowns out the sounds of the world. Once you recognize His voice you'll never want to go back. Your ears will be tuned to a higher calling.

It's a call from stress to rest.

2

THE GREAT STRUGGLE

How would you respond if I asked, "Name the greatest battles which have ever been fought"? Would you cite the Civil War? World War II? Vietnam?

Each of these conflicts merit their place in history, yet the paramount skirmishes of our world have not been waged to conquer empires or vanquish enemies. No. They are being fought every day within the heart of man.

It's a constant struggle between good and evil, between righteousness and sin, between God and Satan.

Who's in Charge?

The Apostle Paul described the forces that were tearing at his heart and soul when he wrote: "For we know that the law is spiritual: but I am carnal, sold under sin. For that which I do I allow not: for what I would, that do I not; but what I hate, that do I. If then I do that which I

The Great Struggle

would not, I consent unto the law that it is good. Now then it is no more I that do it, but sin that dwelleth in me" (Romans 7:14-17).

Paul admitted that in his sinful nature he was helpless. He even stated that he had the desire to do what was good, yet could not carry it out. "For the good that I would I do not: but the evil which I would not, that I do" (v.19).

The Apostle found himself hopelessly engulfed by a sea of sin.

How does he explain the fact that his actions betray the person he should be? Paul says it was the "sin that dwelleth in me" (v.20).

Can you identify with the struggle? The picture he paints is exceedingly bleak.

It is man's sinful nature that produces lust, pride, greed, envy, bitterness, jealousy, deceit, malice, and the desire to kill and destroy.

Here's the principle that Paul found working inside him: "When I would do good, evil is present with me" (v.21).

In his inward man, the Apostle delighted in God's law, "But I see another law in my members, warring against the law of my mind, and bringing me into captivity to the law of sin which is in my members" (v.23).

Before the law men had no way of knowing — with the exception of conscience — that they were walking contrary to God's will. It was the law that made sin sinful; and caused an awareness in man to comply.

How does Paul resolve the conflict? "There is therefore now no condemnation to them which are in Christ Jesus, who walk not after the flesh, but after the Spirit. For the law of the Spirit of life in Christ Jesus hath made me free from the law of sin and death" (Romans 8:1-2).

In these important verses Paul establishes the fact that we do not have to live under the tyranny of sin and death since in Christ we are dead to the law.

Death cancels all obligation to sin, and because we are Christians we are also dead to iniquity.

Breaking the Law

The simple fact is that you can't keep the law because of sin. Paul said "I am crucified with Christ: nevertheless I live; yet not I, but Christ liveth in me: and the life which I now live in the flesh I live by the faith of the Son of God, who loved me, and gave himself for me" (Galatians 2:20).

When Jesus was nailed to the Cross it was for *my* sins, not His. Christ's death became *my* death. The moment I accepted the Savior I was dead to sin. What does that mean? It means that as far as I am concerned, sin might as well not exist. I am living *in* the world, but not *of* the world.

The Great Struggle

As I like to say, "I'm wrapped up, tangled up, tied up in Jesus." Thank God, sin has no power over me!

I can identify with Jesus when He said, "the prince of this world cometh, and hath nothing in me" (John 14:30).

Before I accepted Christ in my heart by faith; I was weary, worn and sad. He not only took my sin away; I found in Him a resting place.

You may ask, "Preacher, are you saying that you *can't* sin?"

No. That's not what I'm telling you.

If you ask, however, "Can we live free from sin?" the answer is "Yes!"

There is a great difference between the practice of iniquity and dealing with the issue of "if" we sin. I'm not talking about hypocrites, but saints.

If we sin we can go to the One who died to redeem us, who rose to justify us and ascended to intercede for us.

Christ is seated at the right hand of the Father and His blood is on the altar of the Holy of Holiest. Scripture declares, "If we confess our sins, he is faithful and just to forgive us our sins, and to cleanse us from all unrighteousness" (1 John 1:9).

When you say "Father I'm sorry. God, forgive me,"

Jesus will point to His blood, and He will free you. The struggle is not with the law. The law is Holy. And as a child of God you don't have to wrestle with sin. You are dead to sin and sin is dead to you.

No Longer Condemned

Are you among those who walk not after the flesh, but after the Spirit? Or are you still living under condemnation?

Every time a preacher or evangelist gives an altar call, does guilt and self-reproach pull you to the altar? If so, something is wrong! You're not walking in the Spirit.

Remember, Paul says, "I can't keep the law. I find myself doing the things the law condemns me for." But then he writes. "For what the law could not do, in that it was weak through the flesh, God sending his own Son in the likeness of sinful flesh, and for sin, condemned sin in the flesh: That the righteousness of the law might be fulfilled in us, who walk not after the flesh, but after the Spirit" (Romans 8:3-4).

When you are in the Spirit and the Spirit dwells in you, you'll be able to fulfil the law, even as our Master did. "For they that are after the flesh do mind the things of the flesh; but they that are after the Spirit the things of the Spirit. For to be carnally minded is death; but to be spiritually minded is life and peace" (vv.5-6).

Do you truly desire to win the battle that rages inside? Listen to Paul as he says, "Walk in the Spirit, and ye shall not fulfil the lust of the flesh" (Galatians 5:16).

Why is this essential? "Because the carnal mind is enmity against God: for it is not subject to the law of God, neither indeed can be. So then they that are in the flesh cannot please God" (Romans 8:7-8).

Your passion to please the Lord is a vital factor in finding peace and rest. It's a two step process.

First, we come to Him by faith. Second, we retain our unbroken fellowship with Him by obedience.

That is what is pleasing to God.

The choice is clear. "But ye are not in the flesh, but in the Spirit, if so be that the Spirit of God dwell in you. Now if any man have not the Spirit of Christ, he is none of his" (.v.9).

If you have the Spirit of Christ, you belong to Him. And remember this: The Lord is *for* you, not against you! If He was for you when you were a no-good sinner, do you think He is going to turn His back on you now? "If Christ be in you, the body is dead because of sin; but the Spirit is life because of righteousness" (v.10).

It is sin that kills the body — and it is going to die unless Jesus comes back and changes it from mortal to immortality. But thank God the soul to whom He promised rest has already been resurrected from spiritual death and is alive. "But if the Spirit of him that raised up Jesus from the dead dwell in you, he that raised up Christ from the dead shall also quicken your mortal bodies by his Spirit that dwelleth in you" (v.11).

Where does the Spirit dwell? Not *around* you, but *in* you! Despite the deadness of the body the Spirit of God is within and you are spiritually alive. Your soul has been raised from spiritual death.

Your Glorified Body

If Jesus tarries your body is going back to the dust of the earth. However, if you are a new creature in Christ, you will ascend on high to your Heavenly Father and await the return of the Lord to be reunited with that body. It will not be the mortal shell that went into the grave. It will be a resurrected, *glorified* body.

Forever, you will have peace and rest.

All this is possible because you responded to the Divine invitation to be raised from spiritual death. Jesus said, "I am the resurrection, and the life: he that believeth in me, though he were dead, yet shall he live: And whosoever liveth and believeth in me shall never die" (John 11:25-26)

What we're talking about surpasses anything Adam ever experienced. He lived in a mortal body. But because of the Second Adam from above our bodies shall be raised from death.

While we await the glorious return of Christ, we are

to walk in obedience with our Redeemer so that sin no longer holds any attraction to us. In the words of Paul, "I count all things but loss for the excellency of the knowledge of Christ Jesus my Lord: for whom I have suffered the loss of all things, and do count them but dung, that I may win Christ." (Philippians 3:8).

Make no mistake. The struggle between the flesh and the Spirit is real. Only through Jesus can we claim victory.

3

"WHERE CAN I FIND PEACE?"

Americans are spending billions in a mad rush for self protection. They buy elaborate electronic security systems and install huge dead-bolt locks on their doors until their homes resemble an armed fortress.

In their quest for physical safety, however, they have ignored the true cause of their fear and insecurity. They have not found peace in their heart.

There are countless causes for such anxiety. We feel threatened by circumstances, conditions and people. Often these problems arise from emotional instability that has developed since childhood.

Just because we emphasize the spiritual we can't ignore the natural. We must recognize and deal with life accordingly. We are three-fold beings — spirit, soul and body — and the Lord is concerned about the whole man.

Here's what Paul wrote to the Christians at Thessalonica: "And the very God of peace sanctify you wholly; and I pray God your whole spirit and soul and body be preserved blameless unto the coming of our Lord Jesus Christ" (1 Thessalonians 5:23).

What kind of God do we serve? A "God of peace."

If you are struggling with emotional and relational problems, take comfort in the fact that if you profess faith in Jesus, you have access to the true source of peace.

Internal Security

What happened to you in your childhood doesn't need to dictate the quality of your life today. Why? Because you have been raised from spiritual death through the New Birth.

Countless people have been brain-washed and programmed by negative messages. They've been told: "You'll never amount to anything!" "You're a loser!" "You're no good!"

As a result of this constant bombardment, their self-esteem has been severely damaged.

Many parents have given their children adequate food, shelter and clothing, yet they have failed to feed their vision and wrap them in self-confidence.

Making a child feel loved, wanted and important is vital. If peace and security are not prevalent in the home the neglected individual will turn to his peers, searching for a substitute.

When a young person feels bonded with his family, the pressures from the outside will have little affect on his values. That's why God says, "Train up a child in the way he should go: and when he is old, he will not depart from it"(Proverbs 22:6).

Your children may drift away and taste of the world for a season, but they're not going to be satisfied. Especially if you have instilled in them the power of love.

Regardless of how you were programmed, with God's help, you can rise above it. "For whatsoever is born of God overcometh the world: and this is the victory that overcometh the world, even our faith" (1 John 5:4).

In the arms of Christ we find peace, security and fellowship.

What you may have missed in a natural family can be more than compensated by a personal relationship with Christ and the love of your spiritual family.

You will experience the joyous, abundant life Jesus promised. He declared, "The thief cometh not, but for to steal, and to kill, and to destroy: I am come that they might have life, and that they might have it more abundantly" (John 10:10).

When you know deep in your soul that you are at peace with God, it makes no difference what people may say. You feel internally satisfied because you have a clean, pure heart. The past is buried and you are ready for a marvelous new life.

He Understands

A woman recently lamented, "You don't understand. You don't know what I'm going through!"

I responded, "You're right. I may not know, but I have a friend who does. Jesus knows."

Regardless of what you are facing, Christ has traveled that road. Scripture declares, "For we have not an high priest which cannot be touched with the feeling of our infirmities; but was in all points tempted like as we are, yet without sin" (Hebrews 4:15).

Not only has He walked through your crisis, He conquered it. "These things I have spoken unto you, that in me ye might have peace. In the world ye shall have tribulation: but be of good cheer; I have overcome the world" (John 16:33).

If you want to discover perfect peace, enter into His presence — knowing that His very nature is rest. Jesus was speaking directly to you when He said, "Peace I leave with you, my peace I give unto you: not as the world giveth, give I unto you. Let not your heart be troubled, neither let it be afraid" (John 14:27).

Yoked With Him

Every day I praise God that I am yoked with the Prince of Peace. We are so close that we have become one — nothing separates Jesus and me.

- Thank God I'm called to preach. But preaching doesn't come before Jesus.
- Thank God I can pray. But praying doesn't come before Jesus.
- Thank God I can sing under the anointing. But nothing takes the place of my fellowship with Jesus.

You see, He woke me up this morning and started me on my way. And if Jesus isn't there, I can't pray. If Jesus isn't there, I can't preach. If Jesus isn't there, I can't sing. It simply becomes sounding brass or tinkling cymbals. Oh, I might open my mouth and make a noise, yet if the Lord isn't there the words will never touch a hungry soul.

Even more important, if Jesus isn't there I can't have peace.

A Stream in the Desert

There is a place of quiet rest near to the heart of God. As the Psalmist wrote: God is our refuge and strength, a very present help in trouble. Therefore will not we fear, though the earth be removed, and though the mountains be carried into the midst of the sea; Though the waters thereof roar and be troubled, though the mountains shake with the swelling thereof. There is a river, the streams whereof shall make glad the city of God, the holy place of the tabernacles of the most High" (Psalms 46:1-4).

The Lord can create a sea of tranquility in the midst of darkness and disaster. Out of the rocky, dry land He can create an oasis in the desert.

Where is that stream? Jesus says, "He that believeth on me, as the scripture hath said, out of his belly shall flow rivers of living water" (John 7:38).

You are invited to drink from this well that will never run dry. Are you weary? Are you heavy laden? Are you oppressed and sad? The "Spirit and the bride say, Come. And let him that heareth say, Come. And let him that is athirst come. And whosoever will, let him take the water of life freely" (Revelation 22:17).

From my personal experience and from God's Holy Word let me assure you that you can know "the peace of God, which passeth all understanding"(Philippians 4:7).

He is the only security you'll ever need.

4

AN AWESOME TRANSFORMATION

You can kneel at an altar of repentance a thousand times. You can make enough promises to God to fill a book. You can shed tears until your pillow is moist. Yet if you continue to live in sin and immorality something's drastically wrong.

It's not your remorse or your regret that brings salvation. The great transformation you seek only happens when the blood of Christ is applied to your heart.

How will you know the work is done? You will not only believe, you'll *behave!*

Without doubt, God desires to sanctify you Holy. He also wants to sanctify you *wholly* — from the top of your head to the soles of your feet. It will affect the steps you make and the actions you take.

What does "holiness" mean? It signifies that you have been set apart unto Godliness. From the moment you commence on the journey with your Heavenly Father you will never be the same.

It's not your talents, abilities, or how much money you have in your checkbook that impresses the Lord. If you are not walking by His side in righteousness your life is nothing more than a sham, a facade — like the fake front of a Hollywood movie set. It is hollow.

You can't mix oil and water. How can you sing in the choir on Sunday after "shucking and jiving" at the club on Saturday night?

When you are "playing" church you're really not deluding anyone but yourself. Even more tragically, you are living beneath your privilege.

A "Living Sacrifice"

What is the secret of attaining righteousness?

What does it take for a total transformation?

Scripture holds the key. I pray the Lord will cause these words to be emblazoned in your mind and heart: "I beseech you therefore, brethren, by the mercies of God,

An Awesome Transformation

that ye present your bodies a living sacrifice, holy, acceptable unto God, which is your reasonable service. And be not conformed to this world: but be ye transformed by the renewing of your mind, that ye may prove what is that good, and acceptable, and perfect, will of God" (Romans 12:1-2).

Sadly, our minds have been programmed to think as the world thinks. Even worse, our behavior is affected; we mimic the activities of the world.

- Just because celebrities have glamorized drugs and alcohol doesn't mean you have to follow them.
- Just because your friends are addicted to nicotine doesn't force you to smoke.
- Just because they're handing out condoms at your high school doesn't mean you should become promiscuous.

Regardless of the pressures you may face; in spite of how hopeless or helpless you feel; stop searching for answers in all the wrong places. Stand still and see the salvation of the Lord.

Your Secret Strength

Don't sell yourself short. You have more power than

you ever envisioned. You can present your body as a living sacrifice because of the supernatural authority and strength of the Person who is living inside. He is more powerful than any force that may be oppressing you.

My Bible declares, "Ye are of God, little children, and have overcome them: because greater is he that is in you, than he that is in the world"(1 John 4:4).

Your ultimate success in life is not because you are tall, dark and handsome. It doesn't rely on the stylish fashions you wear, the sporty car in the driveway or the title on your office door. No. The final victory is possible only when you've been changed from death to life and God becomes alive in your soul.

It's time to put distance between yourself and the world. Scripture tells you to "Come out from among them, and be ye separate, saith the Lord, and touch not the unclean thing; and I will receive you" (2 Corinthians 6:17).

The darts and arrows aimed in your direction will be meaningless when you hear a voice from heaven saying, "I am your Father and you are my child."

It's been said that "home is where the heart is," and if

you have been washed in His blood, you have a brand new dwelling place. And to prove that you are truly a son or daughter of God, the Lord has reserved a great inheritance for you. It is held this moment in an eternal escrow under your name. The mortgage to your heavenly home is paid in full! You are "heirs of God, and joint-heirs with Christ" (Romans 8:17).

No Need to Wait

While you rejoice about the fact that you have a mansion being built on a street paved with gold, don't overlook the fact that God is standing at the balcony of heaven waiting to pour out His blessings today. Why wait? He's a "right now" God — a *present* help in time of trouble.

- He's my joy when I am sad.
- He's my friend when I am lonely.
- He's my physician when I am sick.
- He's my bread when I am hungry.
- He's my water when I am thirsty.
- He's my peace in the midst of a storm.
- He's my rest when I am weary.

If you're looking for a friend that will stay closer than a brother; who will never leave you or forsake you; who is the same yesterday today and forever, I recommend my

Lord to you. He's God Almighty and He will never change.

The Lord doesn't love you because you are good, because you are worthy or because you conform. He loves you because He is love.

Others may disappoint or betray you, yet God embraces you just as you are. And He will never, never let you down. If you falter, He will lift you up and establish your goings. If you are stalked by Satan, He will be your hiding place.

He is *always* there!

Listen to how the Psalmist described your ever-present Father. "Whither shall I go from thy spirit? Or whither shall I flee from thy presence? If I ascend up into heaven, thou art there: if I make my bed in hell, behold, thou art there. If I take the wings of the morning, and dwell in the uttermost parts of the sea; Even there shall thy hand lead me, and thy right hand shall hold me" (Psalms 139:7-10).

That's right! Even before you arrive, God is present. That is why the Apostle Paul could stand on Mars Hill and declare to the people of Athens, "For in him we live, and move, and have our being" (Acts 17:28).

Making it Permanent

I've met scores of people who have signed a membership card, yet they have never met the *Head* of the church. They're religious all right — religious about the pastor, the evangelist or the denomination — sadly, they haven't been reborn. They have not made Jesus the object of their faith, love and worship. These misguided people are missing the whole purpose of the church. The church is simply a channel to bring people to Christ.

It is Jesus that makes the change.

How does the transformation become permanent? How does righteousness remain? There is only one answer; you need to stay in touch with God — and shut out the distractions that would block your view. The Word declares, "Blessed is the man that walketh not in the counsel of the ungodly, nor standeth in the way of sinners, nor sitteth in the seat of the scornful" (Psalms 1:1).

You don't live for God because of the preacher's exhortations or your parent's expectations. You live in holiness because you trust in the Savior, delight yourself in Him and commit to His will.

You meditate on Him day and night — constantly renewing your mind until your thoughts are no longer focused on the world. Your compass is fixed on God.

Thousands of sermons have been preached from the

FROM STRESS TO REST

words of the Psalmist, who wrote:

- Trust in the Lord, and do good; so shalt thou dwell in the land, and verily thou shalt be fed. (Psalms 37:3).
- Delight thyself also in the Lord, and he shall give thee the desires of thine heart (v.4).
- Commit thy way unto the Lord trust also in him; and he shall bring it to pass (v.5).

However, we often overlook what the Psalmist said next. After admonishing us to *trust, delight* and *commit*, he tells us to *rest*. "Rest in the Lord and wait patiently for him" (Psalms 37:7).

How will you know that the great transformation is complete? You'll have peace and harmony. You will rest in Him.

5

DON'T SETTLE FOR SUBSTITUTES

It doesn't take a genius to recognize the miracle-working power of God. You only have to hold a newborn baby or stand before a majestic mountain to know that a higher force fashioned the universe and created man.

God alone should be the object of our worship, yet there are many who are settling for substitutes — drugs, alcohol, money, fame or personal gain. That's why the Word asks: "Examine yourselves, whether ye be in the faith" (2 Corinthians 13:5).

Where are You Looking?

The *rest* promised by the Lord does not reside in a system, in society, or in religion — it is only found in the Lord. It's true of both individuals and of governments.

FROM STRESS TO REST

As a nation, Israel rejected the Almighty and was scattered abroad to suffer persecution, oppression and anguish. It first happened at the hand of Nebuchadnezzar, the King of Babylon.

When his troops invaded the Holy City of Israel, they "burnt the house of the Lord, and the king's house, and all the houses of Jerusalem, and every great man's house burnt he with fire. And all the army of the Chaldees, that were with the captain of the guard, brake down the walls of Jerusalem round about" (2 Kings 25:9-10).

Centuries later, Jesus spoke of the end times, saying, "And they shall fall by the edge of the sword, and shall be led away captive into all nations: and Jerusalem shall be trodden down of the Gentiles, until the times of the Gentiles be fulfilled" (Luke 21:24).

Christ extended the invitation for Israel to come to Him and find rest. He entered the synagogues and told religious leaders to halt their ritualistic laws and practices. The Messiah for whom they sought so long was in their midst, yet they rejected Him.

According to Scripture, after the church age, at the end of the tribulation period, God's chosen people will be restored.

If Israel as a nation had accepted their Messiah, they would not have been scattered throughout the earth and suffered such great persecution. It was only after their rejection of Christ that God grafted the Gentiles into the olive tree as a branch.

The offer still remains. Both Jew and Gentile can find rest in their soul through Jesus. "But as many as received him, to them gave he power to become the sons of God, even to them that believe on his name" (John 1:12).

Faith or Fraud?

Scripture tells us that in the last days people will be beguiled by those who pretend to have God's power. Jesus said, "Take heed that ye be not deceived: for many shall come in my name, saying, I am Christ; and the time draweth near: go ye not therefore after them" (Luke 21:8).

Many will be swayed by the "man of sin" that will come upon the world scene. They will be drawn to his so-called supernatural spectaculars and fall at his feet.

> **Only a heart that is in tune with the Holy Spirit has the discernment to know the difference between faith and fraud.**

How can you know the genuine from the counterfeit?

How can you avoid being the victim of a spiritual charlatan?

Ground yourself in the Word until your foundation is so deep that no storm will ravage you. God says, "My people are destroyed for lack of knowledge: because thou hast rejected knowledge, I will also reject thee, that thou shalt be no priest to me: seeing thou hast forgotten the law of thy God, I will also forget thy children" (Hosea 4:6).

Do you want to know how to study the Word? "For precept must be upon precept, precept upon precept; line upon line, line upon line; here a little, and there a little" (Isaiah 28:10).

I make no apology for preaching the same message again and again. God knows our ability to comprehend and retain His wisdom.

The Word must be read, memorized and repeated until it penetrates our mind and heart.

It takes self-discipline to read the Scriptures on a systematic basis. Yet the study of God's Word is more important than any daily routine you can name.

"I Don't Feel Like It"

Is it any wonder so many people have stress when they are living by feelings?

They roll over on Sunday morning and moan, "I don't feel like going to church. I'm tired, and besides, I don't feel very spiritual today."

Well, salvation has to do with faith, not feelings. There may be times when you pray and the heavens seem like brass. It doesn't mean that God has abandoned you.

Satan will take advantage of such an opportunity and attempt to convince you that you've sinned — to the extent that the Lord doesn't even hear you. The devil delights when your emotions become a substitute for God's sovereignty.

You'll Never Move Me!

Not only do we need to come to Jesus; we need to firmly establish our faith. Regardless of what we may feel at the moment, our confidence in Christ must be unshakable. We must move to the place where we can say with Paul, "For I know whom I have believed, and am persuaded that he is able to keep that which I have committed unto him against that day" (2 Timothy 1:12).

You see, Paul had been whipped, stoned, imprisoned and was ready to die for the cause of Christ. As he prepared to face his accusers, he boldly declared, "But none of these things move me, neither count I my life dear unto myself, so that I might finish my course with joy, and the ministry, which I have received of the Lord Jesus, to testify the gospel of the grace of God" (Acts 20:24).

Paul wasn't a doubter like Thomas who said, "Except I shall see in his hands the print of the nails, and put my finger into the print of the nails, and thrust my hand into his side, I will not believe" (John 20:25).

He didn't run and hide like Peter when Christ was being accused. Peter lied, "I do not know the man" (Matthew 26:72).

Not Paul. His confidence wasn't based on feelings. He had been tested by fire and knew God was God.

The Road Home

I pity the backslider. He made a commitment he no longer wants to keep; he drifts away in his carnal state and searches for answers in a depraved, corrupt world. It's not long, however, until he comes to the realization that he cannot substitute natural remedies for spiritual needs.

At every turn of the road it seems someone is witnessing to him. He turns on the radio and hears a Gospel song — and wonders if it is just coincidence. He clicks on the television and suddenly someone is preaching. He feels the words are directed at him.

Perhaps he has succeeded financially, yet his soul is troubled and he can't enjoy his achievement. He tries to sleep, but these words keep ringing in his ears:

> *"For what is a man profited, if he shall gain the whole world, and lose his own soul? or what shall a man give in exchange for his soul?"*
> — Matthew 16:26.

The day finally comes when he realizes that pleasure quickly passes and possessions have fleeting value. Like the prodigal son, he says, "I've had it! I'm going home to my father."

Jesus is waiting with open arms, saying, "Welcome. I will give you rest."

There aren't a thousand roads to heaven. Only one. Jesus said, "I am the way, the truth, and the life: no man cometh unto the Father, but by me" (John 14:6).

Your eternal soul is far too valuable to entrust with counterfeits, copies and imitations.

There's no substitute for the Savior.

6

REST IN THE SPIRIT

Long before Christ came to earth, God knew that man needed to communicate with Him on a level that was beyond human understanding. He would speak to His children in a new tongue — and it would bring rest and refreshing to those who received it.

The prophet Isaiah declared: "For with stammering lips and another tongue will he speak to this people" (Isaiah 28:11).

God also spoke through His servant Joel, saying, "And it shall come to pass . . . that I will pour out my spirit upon all flesh; and your sons and your daughters shall prophesy, your old men shall dream dreams, your young men shall see visions" (Joel 2:28).

The fulfillment of those prophesies came to pass when

Christ ascended into heaven. Just before He returned to His Father, Jesus told the disciples, "It is expedient for you that I go away: for if I go not away, the Comforter will not come unto you; but if I depart, I will send him unto you" (John 16:7).

The Lord didn't promise a judge or a critic, but a *Comforter*.

Help from Above

What did Jesus say the Holy Spirit would do?

- He will "dwell in you" (John 14:17).
- He will "teach you all things" (v.16).
- He will "bring all things to your remembrance, whatsoever I have said to you" (v, 26).
- He "shall testify of me." (V.26).
- He is "the Spirit of truth" (v.17).
- He will "abide with you forever" (v.16).

Even more, Christ promised that the Comforter would energize and empower every believer. "But ye shall receive power, after that the Holy Ghost is come upon you: and ye shall be witnesses unto me both in Jerusalem, and in all Judaea, and in Samaria, and unto the uttermost part of the earth" (Acts 1:8).

Those were the last recorded words of Christ before

He was taken up into heaven.

On the day of Pentecost about one hundred and twenty believers gathered in the Upper Room to await the promise of the Father. They were filled with anticipation because Christ had said, "For John truly baptized with water; but ye shall be baptized with the Holy Ghost not many days hence" (Acts 1:5).

What a meeting that must have been! They didn't need a worship leader, or an organ or piano. There was no one entertaining them. The room was filled with expectation and they were praising God.

Suddenly, the Spirit descended like a fire, "And they were all filled with the Holy Ghost, and began to speak with other tongues, as the Spirit gave them utterance" (Acts 2:4).

When those Spirit-filled believers walked out of the Upper Room there was an explosion of great joy. A mighty revival broke out in Jerusalem.

Thousands were brought into the Kingdom and the news spread throughout the known world.

Rest in the Spirit

It's Still Available

The same Spirit that fell on the early church is here today. It was not for a special dispensation that ended with the Apostles.

There are times when words fail us and we can't adequately express what is in our heart. That's where the Spirit comes in.

The Apostle Paul wrote, "Likewise the Spirit also helpeth our infirmities: for we know not what we should pray for as we ought: but the Spirit itself maketh intercession for us with groanings which cannot be uttered" (Romans 8:26).

If you are confused and burdened, enter into your prayer closet and shut the door. Tell the Lord, "I won't come out until you speak to my soul." Start praying and God will take over — often with words you may not understand.

I challenge you to surrender totally to Him — with every fiber of your being. He will edify and build you in the Most Holy faith.

When you pray in the Holy Ghost, the Spirit reveals Jesus, allowing Christ to meet your needs.

You may ask, "How do I begin?"

Start by exalting and praising Jesus — then allow the Holy Spirit to praise Him *through* you. That's all you have to do.

- Look at your Red Sea. It is Jesus who will cause the waters to part.
- Look at your fiery furnace. It is Jesus who extinguishes the flame.
- Look at your Goliath. It is Jesus who defeats your giants.
- Look at your lion's den. It is Jesus who locks the jaws of your enemies.

Start praising Him. Start worshiping Him. Begin thanking Him for all He has done. At that very moment the Spirit is interceding on your behalf. He takes the message from your heart and delivers it to the Father through Jesus.

When you are praying in the Holy Ghost, you become lost in Him — worshiping in a heavenly language.

Your tears will turn to delight. "Weeping may endure for a night, but joy cometh in the morning" (Psalms 30:5).

Every Day!

You may ask, "How often should I pray in the Spirit?" Every day of your life!

God's heart must be grieved by people who call themselves Christians, yet their time with Him is limited to an occasional church service at Easter or Mother's Day. However, you don't need to enter the sanctuary to be refreshed. You can feast on the Word and pray in the Spirit anywhere, any moment, any day.

Spend time with the Holy Spirit. After all, the Holy Spirit can only use what you make available. Jesus said, "Man shall not live by bread alone, but by every word that proceedeth out of the mouth of God" (Matthew 4:4).

How can you be fed by the Spirit if you're not in His presence?

When the Holy Spirit is at work, you won't need to unwind because you won't get uptight.

Should night overtake you, the Comforter can bring daylight. Remember, it was the Spirit of God that caused the sun to stand still so that Joshua could finish the battle.

When you are surrounded by the protecting power of the Holy Spirit you have a strong defense again Satan.

Don't Stop Now

What about the person who has once experienced the baptism of the Holy Spirit and rejects it? What about the man or woman who once had a beautiful prayer language but no longer exercises spiritual gifts?

I say this as kindly and as humbly as I know how. The person who backs away from their experience in the Holy Spirit and refuses to edify the Lord in their private devotion by praying in other tongues, will live with anxiety, confusion, and frustration.

When pressures mount they don't know how to respond. When Satan attacks, they've lost the power that can command him to flee.

There are times when you are troubled and perplexed and you don't seem to know why. The Holy Spirit understands. Let Him quietly take your burden to the Lord.

Isn't it time you begin to rest in the Holy Spirit? The Comforter has come!

7

THE FAITH FACTOR

Before God spoke creation into existence, He had you and me in mind. The Creator knew far in advance that those who receive His Son by faith will come to a place of rest in Him.

What about those who have not trusted Christ? They find no peace and contentment because they are not meeting God's conditions.

Paul shares with the believers at Galatia how he lives the Christian life. He declares, "I am crucified with Christ: nevertheless I live; yet not I, but Christ liveth in me: and the life which I now live in the flesh I live by the faith of the Son of God, who loved me, and gave himself for me" (Galatians 2:20).

How does Paul live in Christ? By *faith!*

Essential Ingredients

There is a great principle in the New Testament that

explains why Israel did not enter into the rest God promised. Here it is: *God's message of redemption must be combined with faith.*

The Apostle, writing to the Hebrews, declares that the offer still stands — and we'd better not miss it. He says, "Let us therefore fear, lest, a promise being left us of entering into his rest, any of you should seem to come short of it" (Hebrews 4:1).

Paul establishes the fact that the Gospel which was being preached in his day was the same message that was given through the prophets. But why did it produce such limited results in ancient times? It was not combined with faith. He states: "For unto us was the gospel preached, as well as unto them: but the word preached did not profit them, not being mixed with faith in them that heard it" (v.2).

Quoting from the Old Testament (Psalms 95:11), Paul makes it clear that those who forsake God's ways, "shall not enter my rest."

Sustaining Life

It's been said that "some eat to live and others live to eat!"

Regardless of which is true, we partake of food because it is necessary — our bodies must be sustained. God has given us an appetite for natural food. We eat it, chew it and it enters our body.

What happens next? The food is mixed with digestive juices that cause it to be assimilated into our blood stream, tissue and cells. Suddenly, the nutrients are working to fortify us for another day.

If food is not properly combined with the digestive juices our life would be in mortal danger.

It's very similar with God's Word. The message must be mixed with faith.

Earlier, we established the fact that we are soul, spirit and body. The first two constitute the inner man — which is sustained by spiritual means.

> *It makes little difference how well you feed or pamper the body — the natural man — it will return to the dust of the earth.*

The inner man, however, can be fed with God's Word. If it is absorbed and digested, our spirit and soul goes home to be with the Lord.

It's not necessary to make the Word more palatable. Feast upon it just as it is. After all, God said what He meant and meant what He said.

The Creator knew what our needs would be for time and eternity. So we don't simply *read* the Word, we absorb it into our heart and being. We combine it with faith and are forever strengthened in the inner man.

He's Not Resting!

Paul's message includes the fact that "God did rest the seventh day from all his works." (Hebrews 4:4).

Only *once* did God rest, and since that time He has been increasingly busy bringing man back to Himself — following through on His plan to restore creation to its original state. His Son declared: "Behold, I stand at the door, and knock: if any man hear my voice, and open the door, I will come in to him, and will sup with him, and he with me" (Revelation 3:20).

We are instructed to rest on the Sabbath day, but God will not stop His work until every person possible accepts His salvation by faith.

At the end of the Millennium — the thousand years in which the Lord Jesus will reign on the planet and bring all things under subjection — the dead shall be raised from the grave. Scripture says the world will be judged and those who follow Satan will be cast into the lake of fire. The devil and his demons will be forever vanquished. There will be no more sin on earth and death will be canceled.

That's when we will enter into the final phase of eternal rest on the planet earth.

Paul spoke of that time when he wrote: "Seeing therefore it remaineth that some must enter therein, and they to whom it was first preached entered not in because of unbelief" (Hebrews 4:6).

The Faith of Abraham

The Gospel — including the message of faith — was given to Abraham 430 years before the law. The Bible records that "the scripture, foreseeing that God would justify the heathen through faith, preached before the gospel unto Abraham, saying, In thee shall all nations be blessed" (Galatians 3:8).

Paul points out that not all of Abrahams's children are truly Israel (Romans 9:6). Some became "the children of promise" (v.8).

When the Lord preached to Abraham, He set forth His plan for you and me. God said, "I will bless them that bless thee, and curse him that curseth thee: and in thee shall all families of the earth be blessed" (Genesis 12:3).

Abraham. What a story! He was called out from a heathen family in a heathen nation by a God whom neither he or his people knew or recognized.

The Lord looked into Abraham's heart and recognized his potential for righteousness. He not only had faith, he was faithful.

FROM STRESS TO REST

God told Abraham that through his seed all nations would be blessed. Yet he and his wife, Sarah, were well beyond child-bearing years.

The promise, however, was not predicated on Abraham's ability to produce or the condition of Sarah's womb. God said He would give them a son and that's exactly what happened.

Mary, the mother of Jesus, came from the seed of Abraham.

How was it possible for the "father of all nations" to enter into God's rest, yet Israel did not? Abraham chose to live by faith.

It's Your Decision

I was once asked, "Pastor, does the Gospel provide a plan whereby some people are going to be saved and some lost? Will some go to heaven or hell in spite of themselves?"

Without hesitation, I answered, "No. A thousand times, no!"

Paul made that clear when he wrote: "For this is good and acceptable in the sight of God our Savior; who will have all men to be saved, and to come unto the knowledge of the truth" (1 Timothy 2:3-4).

The Apostle Peter was just as clear on the matter. He declared: "The Lord is not slack concerning his promise,

The Faith Factor

as some men count slackness; but is longsuffering to us-ward, not willing that any should perish, but that all should come to repentance" (2 Peter 3:9).

The decision is *yours!*

Who enters God's rest? Those who accept Christ by faith.

8

WHO CAN YOU TRUST?

I can remember the time when you could place total trust in a man — his word was his bond.

- A customer could walk into a bank and receive a loan simply on a handshake.
- The owner of the corner store would allow a customer to take home a bag of groceries, knowing the bill would be settled on payday.
- A man could borrow literally anything from his neighbor.

Why was this possible? Because men and women were faithful to their word. They could be relied upon.

Today, confidence and trust have been replaced with suspicion and doubt. As one man lamented, "I wish I could have faith in people, but I'm wary. I've been burned too many times."

Where is Truth?

If you can't depend on your fellow man, where can you turn? Who can you trust?

I am delighted to tell you that Your Heavenly Father will never deceive or betray you. Scripture tells us, "God is not a man, that he should lie; neither the son of man, that he should repent: hath he said, and shall he not do it? or hath he spoken, and shall he not make it good?" (Numbers 23:19).

I am constantly bewildered by people who express disappointment in the character and integrity of those around them, yet hesitate to lift their eyes toward heaven.

> ***God is exceedingly patient and longsuffering. That is why He has not plunged the world into judgment.***

Sinners who curse and reject their Maker may think they are getting away with it. God is just being merciful. He is giving these misguided individuals a time to recognize that their needs are far beyond the ability of man to heal.

I remember witnessing to a disheveled man who was sitting on a curbside with a cheap bottle of wine clutched in his hand.

"Do you know God," I asked.

"Sure I do," he retorted in his drunken stupor. "I am god."

Immediately, I thought about the verse, "The fool hath said in his heart, There is no God" (Psalms 14:1).

I'm glad that Jesus is at the *mercy seat*, pleading for the world. And there are millions of believers interceding for the lost.

Eventually Christ will step down from the mercy seat and move to the judgment seat — and the world will be thrown into chaos, darkness and death. It's something born again Christians don't have to worry about. We will be with Him.

God is merciful, but the day of salvation will not last forever. Now is the appointed time to place your confidence in Him.

Try the Spirits

Not only can you trust the Father and the Son, you can depend upon God's Spirit.

As a pastor I would love to tell you that every person who enters the sanctuary comes for the purpose of worshiping or to honor and glorify Jesus. No, there are many unclean spirits who come into the church. Often I have to rebuke them before walking to the platform.

John warned: "Beloved, believe not every spirit, but try the spirits whether they are of God: because many false prophets are gone out into the world" (1 John 4:1).

Satan attempts to undermine our faith by using the Word — then will misuse, misinterpret, and take it out of context.

Think about it. If the sly serpent didn't feed you a few morsels of reality, you wouldn't accept anything he says.

The devil captures your trust with truth, then attempts to steal your soul with deception.

There are a variety of godless spirits moving through the land and, sadly, many of them are cloaked in religious garments. They are diverting millions of people from the true road to heaven. Perhaps they've knocked at your door or tried to pin a flower on your lapel at the airport.

Devils in disguise prey on weak, gullible people who are inclined to believe that all religions are good. They don't realize that Jesus is the *only* way.

Buddha, Confucius and Mohammed are dead. Only Christ can say, "I am he that liveth, and was dead; and, behold, I am alive for evermore, Amen; and have the keys of hell and of death" (Revelation 1:18). Only the Lord could declare, "I am Alpha and Omega, the beginning and the end, the first and the last" (Revelation 22:13).

Do you want to know if Jesus is alive? Open your heart and let Him enter. When He makes *you* alive, you'll be able to recognize Him for who He is.

Convicting, Convincing

The Holy Spirit is not an "it" floating around. He is a person — the third person in the Godhead.

Christ spoke about the Spirit in personal terms. "And when he is come, he will reprove the world of sin, and of righteousness, and of judgment" (John 16:8).

The Spirit convicts people and convinces them of their need. And when the church does not recognize and give Him His rightful place, it is out of harmony with God because the Holy Ghost is the administrator of the church.

Jesus said the Spirit would reprove the world of sin, righteousness and judgement:

- "Of sin, because they believe not on me" (John 16:9).
- "Of righteousness, because I go to my Father, and ye see me no more" (v.10).
- "Of judgment, because the prince of this world is judged" (v.11).

Through You and Me

Before we can *rest* in Christ, we must *trust* in Christ. And the Holy Spirit is extending the invitation to every person on the face of the earth.

How does the Holy Spirit say "Come"? Through you and me. He makes us living witnesses by indwelling us.

> **God uses the talents with which we have been entrusted, yet it's not by our skills or our abilities that men become convicted and decide they need Jesus.**

People believe on Christ because of the convicting power of the Comforter.

What did the Lord promise would happen when the Holy Spirit touches our lives? "But ye shall receive power, after that the Holy Ghost is come upon you: and ye shall be witnesses unto me both in Jerusalem, and in all Judaea, and in Samaria, and unto the uttermost part of the earth" (Acts 1:8).

People don't surrender to the Lord because they have confidence in your sincerity or trust your integrity. Men and women accept Christ because of the Holy Spirit who is abiding inside of you.

- It's the Holy Spirit in you that causes you to give out that Gospel tract.
- It's the Holy Spirit in you that imparts an anointing on the words you speak.
- It's the Holy Spirit in you that draws them to the Savior.

There's No Other Way

Those who place their hope in humanity will know only heartache and emptiness. Jesus stands ready to fill that void. He declares, "Blessed are they which do hunger and thirst after righteousness: for they shall be filled" (Matthew 5:6).

Embrace the truth of this grand old hymn:

> *Trust and obey,*
> *For there's no other way.*
> *To be happy in Jesus*
> *But to trust and obey.*

9

CONNECTED TO THE SOURCE

I am old enough to remember the days of the Model-T Ford. And before the electronic ignition was invented, the only way to start the engine was to crank it by hand.

Whether it was raining, freezing cold or blistering hot, you'd see men standing in front of their old "tin lizzies" cranking away. However, if there wasn't a clean connection from the magnate that sparked the fire to the engine, you could crank all day and nothing would happen.

That's how it is with the backslider. They are no longer able to keep on course because their batteries have run dry. They're no longer connected to the source.

The Broken Bridge

Remember, it is the Holy Spirit that convicts man of

his sin and convinces him of his need of the Savior. The Holy Spirit is also sensitive to your response. If you continually reject Him, Scripture says He will leave. God declared, "My spirit shall not always strive with man" (Genesis 6:3).

I realize there are many who contend that once you are in Christ you can never be lost. However, that is contrary to the Scriptural principle that God created us as free moral agents and respects our will.

In the Garden of Eden, Adam and Eve should have never sinned, yet God gave them the option of choosing. Unfortunately, they made the wrong decision.

All of God's covenants are conditional — there's an "if" involved. Jesus said to those who believed on Him, "If ye continue in my word, then are ye my disciples indeed" (John 8:31). They had a choice.

Backsliding is almost always a gradual process. Satan chips away at your spiritual life until it begins to fall apart. Like Samson, you wake up one morning and realize you have lost touch with the source of your power.

In the Wilderness

When the Children of Israel were in the wilderness they provoked the Lord — in spite of His grace and mercy toward them. God fed them with water from a rock and sent manna from the skies, yet their hearts were hardened toward Him. What was their fate? They wandered in the wilderness forty years and perished.

That is why the Psalmist wrote, "Today if ye will hear his voice; Harden not your heart, as in the provocation, and as in the day of temptation in the wilderness" (Psalms 95:7-8).

Many believers are still living the wilderness experience because they have not learned perseverance. As one of my friends states: "If you don't pray, you won't stay. And if you don't fast, you won't last!"

Satan isn't about to let you reach the promised land on a bed of ease. He's going to tempt you on every hand because he is still angry that you escaped his camp. It's vital that we not allow ourselves to become hardened, or take the Word for granted.

Christianity is not a do-it-yourself project. You need an unbroken link to the Master.

There are far too many Christians who are trying to add to their faith — trying to substitute spiritual activity for grace. Never forget, we are not saved *by* works, we're saved that we might *perform* good works. The Word says: "All our righteousnesses are as filthy rags" (Isaiah 64:6).

Our deeds accomplish little in God's Kingdom unless we are united in faith with Christ.

Day by Day

Some people have Sunday religion. Once a week they warm a pew like a little bird perched on it's nest, waiting for the preacher to drop morsels into their mouths. And they wonder why they are undernourished, why they never grow and develop.

They're begging for bread and meat when God has provided heavenly food and spiritual vision for them every day of the week. As a result, they are forfeiting God's blessings. Jesus said, "Search the scriptures; for in them ye think ye have eternal life: and they are they which testify of me" (John 5:39).

Spiritual maturity isn't the result of attending church one day a week. It's the result of daily prayer, daily reading of the Word, and daily renewal.

Instead of waiting to be fed, take action. "Let us therefore come boldly unto the throne of grace, that we may obtain mercy, and find grace to help in time of need" (Hebrews 4:16).

I encounter people who wonder, "Why do I receive so little from the Lord?"

After talking with them for a few minutes I understand the problem. They're not receiving because they are not asking. They're not communicating with the Lord. Scripture says, "Ye have not, because ye ask not" (James 4:2). And Jesus declared, "Ask, and it shall be given you; seek, and ye shall find; knock, and it shall be opened unto you" (Matthew 7:7).

He wants to multiply your greatest desire. The Lord "is able to do exceeding abundantly above all that we ask or think, according to the power that worketh in us" (Ephesians 3:20).

Not only that, but "it is your Father's good pleasure to give you the kingdom" (Luke 12:32). In fact, "No good thing will he withhold from them that walk uprightly" (Psalms 84:11).

Many people are asking, yet they search in the wrong location. They are looking for a handout from the government or a donation from a community agency, not realizing that "Every good gift and every perfect gift is from above, and cometh down from the Father of lights, with whom is no variableness, neither shadow of turning" (James 1:17).

Stay Connected

For some people, it seems that unless they're in a crisis the Lord can't have any fellowship with them. It is only when their backs are up against the wall they turn toward God.

Let me give you some time-tested words of wisdom.

FROM STRESS TO REST

Before you lay your head on your pillow tonight, drop down on your knees and say, "Our father who art in Heaven, hallowed be Thy Name. Lord I thank you for today."

> ***You were created to have fellowship with God. Stay connected. Keep the lines of communication open.***

There is a haven of rest for you in God's heart that the tragedies of the world cannot disturb. That place is in His Son, Christ Jesus.

There may be moments we are shaken by the burdens of some devastating event. However, the Lord is simply calling us closer — where He can speak to our hearts and edify our souls. Suddenly the crisis doesn't seem so painful because earth has no sorrows that heaven cannot heal.

Enjoy It!

There is no excuse for people not living the abundant life that Jesus Christ provided for us. Are you enjoying your salvation? Or are you enduring it?

It may feel as though the weight of the world is resting

on your shoulders. The difficulties you face may loom larger than life itself. Friend, I've been there and am a living witness that God can raise a man from the depths of tragedy to the heights of victory.

I want to tell you *it works!*

Learn to forget the past and press toward the mark for the prize of the high calling in Christ Jesus. And do it with a smile. Paul says, "Rejoice in the Lord alway: and again I say, Rejoice" (Philippians 4:4).

I'm savoring my salvation. I love feasting on the Word and combining it with faith.

Joined with Jesus

You were created for one purpose: to have fellowship with God. That means an unbroken, open line to His throne.

Whether we are standing, walking, sitting or kneeling, we must be yoked with Him.

How valuable is it to be joined with Jesus? Take two pieces of paper. On one list all of your problems. On the other list the promises of God. It won't take long to realize that what the Lord provides far exceeds your needs.

It's totally up to you whether you live with pressure or with peace. The provisions have been made; you must appropriate them by faith and let nothing come between

FROM STRESS TO REST

you and your fellowship with God.

- With all of life's crosses, there is a crown.
- With all of life's trials, there is victory.
- With all of life's tests, there is rest.

There is only one fountain filled with soul-saving blood. There is only one Prince of Peace. Stay connected to the source.

10

"LEARN OF ME"

Before we can reach God's place of quietness, there are two prerequisites:

1. We must be *yoked* with Him.
2. We must *learn* of Him.

Here is what Jesus said: "Take my yoke upon you, and learn of me; for I am meek and lowly in heart: and ye shall find rest unto your souls" (Matthew 11:29).

What does it mean to be yoked with Christ? It means that you are no longer pulling the load by yourself — He is also bearing the burden.

The second requirement for entering His peace is to "learn of me."

Grounded in Faith

To overcome life's trials, abandon yourself to the wisdom of the Lord. Recognize the fact that He is the source of all knowledge.

Do you remember what Nicodemus said when he came to Jesus? "We know that thou art a teacher come from God" (John 3:2).

When you turn your life totally to His care, you'll find He is more than an instructor, He becomes responsible for your well-being.

We can identify with Christ because the Son of God became man. He descended to earth to be "one of us" and to teach us how to live above the problems of our fallen nature.

> *How do you place yourself in a position to learn from Christ? You get close to Him by making Him the object of your love and worship.*

The Apostle Paul told believers that the confusion they faced was because they weren't grounded in the faith. He said many are like children, "tossed to and fro, and carried about by every wind of doctrine"(Ephesians 4:14). They have their "understanding darkened, being alienated from the life of God through the ignorance that is in them, because of the blindness of their heart" (v.18).

I've Been Delivered

I am often asked about the doctrine of deliverance we embrace. Well, deliverance is designed to do just what the word implies — to free us from the Adamic state, and bring us into Christ. Essentially, we are brought from heathenism into spiritual enlightenment.

Jesus makes the difference. He is the teacher who instructs us in the riches of His Father.

However, we must keep our eyes open and our minds focused on the objective of our learning — to become like Christ. If we are "teachable" and obedient, His enabling grace will help us to become like Him.

Christ is the great teacher because He teaches from experience.

- Why can Jesus teach us about obedience? He was submissive to the will of His Father.
- Why can the Lord instruct us in suffering? Because He was nailed to the Cross.
- Why can Christ teach us about meekness? Because He was meek and lowly.
- Why can He teach us about deliverance. Because He was delivered from the grave.

FROM STRESS TO REST

Feelings?

We love the excitement of a great church service, yet we need to be careful not to substitute emotional reaction for spiritual manifestation.

Far too many people allow their feelings to become the dominant factor in their lives. Their "hangups" and emotional problems become barriers to the teaching God intends for them to receive.

Oh, you may like to shout and say a loud "Amen," but that's not the goal of preaching and expounding the Word. The object is to make you like Jesus.

God gave us a mind so we can think.

If you could flash the inside of me on a screen when I am preaching you'd probably see my soul dancing. Why? Because truth does something to the inner man. I pray constantly, however, that the emotion I feel will be translated into sound doctrine for the edification of the saints.

The Lord quietly instructs us through the Holy Spirit. He wants us to "Be still, and know that I am God" (Psalms 46:10).

It's not your feelings that produce spiritual growth and development. That only comes from sitting at the feet of Jesus.

"Now" People

The message of Christ is practical — it's *applicable*.

I remember when people talked about the "now generation." Well, as believers we are the "now" people because our teacher not only *was*, but *is*.

We are victorious right now. We are overcomers this very moment. We have joy and peace today.

When a person first experiences salvation there is usually a rush of exhilaration that lifts them to the top of the mountain. Then, when they are hit with the realities of life they wonder, "What's happening? Why can't I feel the same joy all the time?"

Friend, the rest God wants you to know is the result of *learning*. It's the only way you can know peace in the midst of sorrow — delight in the midst of despair.

Though we walk through the valley of the shadow of death, we will fear no evil because we are yoked with Him. The valley means nothing because He has taken the sting from death.

We can lift our voices and sing:

> *And He walks with me,*
> *And He talks with me.*
> *And He tells me I am His own.*
> *And the joy we share as we tarry there,*
> *None other has ever known.*

I thank the Lord every day that I am His and He is mine. The least of His will is my greatest desire. As Paul asks, "Who shall separate us from the love of Christ? shall tribulation, or distress, or persecution, or famine, or nakedness, or peril, or sword?" (Romans 8:35).

Paul was so grounded in Christ that he was able to make this great declaration: "We are more than conquerors through him that loved us. For I am persuaded, that neither death, nor life, nor angels, nor principalities, nor powers, nor things present, nor things to come, nor height, nor depth, nor any other creature, shall be able to separate us from the love of God, which is in Christ Jesus our Lord" (vv. 37-39).

He's the Light

There's never a dark moment in Jesus because you know the "Sun of righteousness . . . with healing in his wings" (Malachi 4:2).

- If you're looking for beauty, He's the "lily of the valleys" (Song of Solomon 2:1).
- If you're looking for security, He's the "sure foundation" (Isaiah 28:16).
- If you're looking for strength, He's the "Lion of the tribe of Judah" (Revelation 5:5).
- If you're looking for happiness, He's "joy unspeakable and full of glory" (1 Peter 1:8).

"Learn of Me"

- If you're looking for rest, He's the Son of Peace" (Luke 10:6).

The great desire of Christ is to lift you up, turn you around and place your feet on a solid rock. He has started a good work in you and it will continue until it is completed.

Hear the Lord as He whispers, "Learn of me."

11

YOU'RE BEING PERFECTED!

Have you ever seen a Georgia mule? He's supposed to walk straight down the row and not trample the crop he is plowing.

It doesn't work. He's greedy and never seems to be satisfied. You can bring him out of the stall with a full tummy, yet that old mule is always looking for something else to munch on.

If you don't put blinders on him he's going to spot a weed and plow a crooked line until he finds it. You finally have to put a bit in his mouth so you can keep him on a straight path — not turning to the left or to the right.

Some people are like that Georgia mule. The Word doesn't hold their attention. They say, "I've heard it all before."

They wander off course when it suits their fancy and don't want anything to cramp their lifestyle. Then they wonder why they never meet God's expectation and enter that place of rest.

If we don't follow the Lord voluntarily, He may have to take some drastic measures to capture our attention.

God said, "Joshua, I want you to take these people across the Jordan. But in order to do that they have to spend time in my Word and conform to its teaching." The Lord told him to "observe to do according to all the law, which Moses my servant commanded thee: turn not from it to the right hand or to the left" (Joshua 1:7).

Next God told His servant, "This book of the law shall not depart out of thy mouth; but thou shalt meditate therein day and night, that thou mayest observe to do according to all that is written therein: for then thou shalt make thy way prosperous, and then thou shalt have good success" (v.8).

The Five-Fold Ministry

God has ordained a five-fold ministry for the church — the body of Christ. "And he gave some, apostles; and some, prophets; and some, evangelists; and some, pastors and teachers" (Ephesians 4:11).

Why did the Lord provide these ministries? ""For the perfecting of the saints, for the work of the ministry, for the edifying of the body of Christ" (Ephesians 4:12).

The purpose of this ordinance is not to strengthen believers in a denomination, a theology, or promote a particular doctrine. It is so that believers may become like Christ.

> *As members of His body, we are to be perfected — or corrected — until we are aligned with Him.*

The saints constitute the body of Christ and Jesus is the Head. What is the single objective? To bring the body in harmony with the Head so that it conforms to the stature, the nature and the characteristics of the Head.

Consequently, we must focus our attention on Jesus.

What is the driving force that leads toward perfection? It is love — the foundation on which we are built and the soil in which we grow.

Adam was created as a perfect man; in the image and likeness of God. He became imperfect because of sin and all of us sprang up from that imperfection — flawed and fallible.

Now we look to Jesus, "the author and finisher of our faith" (Hebrews 12:2). He is the blameless, faultless man and we set our gaze upon Him.

To know Christ intimately makes it possible to conform to His likeness. Why? Because when we look upon the Lord with spiritual eyes, we behold a beauty that cannot be comprehended by the natural mind. Deep within our soul we cry, "That's my desire. I want to be like Jesus."

The preaching of the Gospel is designed to help believers conform to the Head of the body — our Lord and Savior, Christ Jesus.

Who Must Increase?

If we want to find fulfillment, come to maturity and find perfection we must humble ourselves and bow at His feet. As the Apostle John said, "He must increase, but I must decrease" (John 3:30).

Find your place in a loving God and allow Him to use you *when* He wants, *where* He wants and *how* He wants.

Remember, we're not trying to impress people with our skills or with our abilities; we're endeavoring to let people see Jesus. And the more we come to know Him, the more we become like Him.

Let me ask a personal question. At your work, in your school, in your neighborhood and in your social life, do people see Jesus in you? Have you become a light to the world, and salt to the earth?

The Gospel is quick and powerful — sharper than a two-edged sword. It performs the spiritual surgery that is necessary to remove defects in the body of Christ. Then the Holy Spirit heals our wounds with His oil of anointing.

> *Never complain about trials and tests. It's God's "operating room" for your perfection.*

James wrote, "My brethren, count it all joy when ye fall into divers temptations" (James 1:2).

Do you love the Lord? Do you feel called by Him. Then thank God for your problems. Scripture tells us that "All things work together for good to them that love God that are called according to his purpose" (Romans 8:28).

How should you respond when your Heavenly Father reaches down and tightens that bit in your mouth? "Thank you, Lord. I don't understand it, but I know you have a purpose."

Whose Church?

The work of the ministry is placed in the body to correct what needs correction and to edify what needs edification. It's a process that helps the body perform to its capacity and become complete.

Are you living up to your potential in Christ? How many souls are in the Kingdom as a result of your effort? What is the specific ministry you are contributing to your church?

I recently received a letter that began, "Pastor, I am a member of your church."

I wanted to tell them, "It's not *my* church. It's *our* church."

Don't put the responsibility on the pastor. God wants everyone in the body to be perfected.

Never, never become satisfied with the work God has called you to perform. When that happens you become complacent and cease to put forth the effort Christ demands.

I'm satisfied with Jesus, but not with my position as a follower of Christ. I want it to improve. I desire to do more. In fact, I'll never be contented until I walk my last mile and I hear God say, "Well done, thou good and faithful servant . . . enter thou into the joy of thy lord" (Matthew 25:21).

I've seen too many people who watch their community

falling apart — yet they continue to rock away in their favorite chair and do nothing. Their family is disintegrating in front of them and they shrug their shoulders saying, "What can I do?"

When you conform to the image of Christ and are being perfected by Him, you will never stop trying. Jesus says, "If ye abide in me, and my words abide in you, ye shall ask what ye will, and it shall be done unto you" (John 15:7).

The Power of Agreement

Thank God we are not alone in the process of being conformed to Christ. Perfection is for the *body* — the entire church.

> *When a problem arises*
> *I challenge you to seek out*
> *another member and say,*
> *"Come on. Let's agree in prayer."*

It's biblical. Jesus declared, "If two of you shall agree on earth as touching any thing that they shall ask, it shall be done for them of my Father which is in heaven" (Matthew 18:19).

You may ask, "Doesn't the Lord have all power in

heaven and earth? Can't He perform the task all alone?"

Of course, He can. However, God wants us to be shaped and strengthened through the unity of fellow believers. That's why Christ says: "Where two or three are gathered together in my name, there am I in the midst of them" (Matthew 18:20).

Remember, God sends people into your life for a purpose. It's His plan for your perfection.

12

Total Rest

The first time I visited the health club for a workout, I thought I was going to die. By the time I finished I was weary and panting for breath.

The next morning my muscles were sore and my whole body was aching. But, oh, what self-discipline and perseverance will do. When some of my fat began to turn to muscle, I felt like a new man.

Anyone who is serious about physical exercise will tell you, "No pain, no gain!"

What about your spiritual strength? Is it developed the same way? Absolutely. As the Apostle Peter declared, suffering comes, "That the trial of your faith, being much more precious than of gold that perisheth, though it be tried with fire, might be found unto praise and honor and glory at the appearing of Jesus Christ" (1 Peter 1:7).

Your "faith muscles" may be tired and you may feel like giving up, but wait. The Lord has promised rest for the weary and joy in the morning.

The Devil's Bluff

The power of Satan is insignificant when compared to God's grace, mercy and love.

When the devil is finally put in the lake of fire, people are going to look down at him and laugh, "Is that what has had me on the run all my life? Why, he's nothing!"

> *Satan is like a bulldog with all of his teeth pulled out. He can bark, run and growl, but the only way he can bite is if you let him.*

Don't let the devil bluff you and cause you to live beneath your privilege.

Some people are just one step away from entering God's rest. Satan, however, has frightened them so often that they seem paralyzed. They allow the rope of safety to slip through their hands instead of tying a knot and hanging on.

To hear some people relate it, life must be tough:

- "I can't get the preacher on the telephone!"
- "My boyfriend hasn't called me in two months. What am I going to do?"
- "You know that letter of prophecy I received last week? Well, I lost it!"
- "I tried to call the prayer chain and all I got was a busy signal"

They moan and groan, ""Nobody loves me. I can't get anyone to come to my rescue"

They're so busy complaining, they fail to hear a small voice whispering, "Lo, I am with you always."

When I was a boy, I was told to "Stop, look, and listen."That's still excellent advice. Jesus said, "My sheep hear my voice, and I know them, and they follow me" (John 10:27).

The Final Rest

The Lord not only promised rest in this world but an *eternal* rest is waiting for those who have accepted Him.

One day we will depart from the stress and anxiety of this sinful, wicked life and rise to be with the Lord.

John the Revelator wrote: "And I heard a voice from heaven saying unto me, Write, Blessed are the dead which die in the Lord from henceforth: Yea, saith the Spirit, that they may rest from their labors" (Revelation 14:13).

The Divine invitation is not temporary, it is for your

continual, permanent deliverance.

> ***What you may suffer in this life is only a passing memory. It will pale when compared with the glory we will share with Him.***

Paul wrote, "For our light affliction, which is but for a moment, worketh for us a far more exceeding and eternal weight of glory" (2 Corinthians 4:17).

The day is quickly approaching when you will stand before the judgment seat of Christ. Your silver, gold, and material possessions will be consumed in flames. The only lasting treasure will be a heart that has been cleansed by His blood and a soul that has found peace through the rest He offers.

"You Ain't Seen Nothin'"

We only pass this way once. It's a probationary period the Lord has granted to prepare us for eternity.

You may have never been greatly acclaimed or granted special recognition. Don't be disappointed. If you have placed your life in the arms of Christ there's a welcome being prepared for you that exceeds any applause this world can offer. In other words, "You ain't seen nothin' yet!"

John says, "Beloved, now are we the sons of God, and it doth not yet appear what we shall be: but we know that, when he shall appear, we shall be like him; for we shall see him as he is" (1 John 3:2).

> *The world beyond isn't full of strange science-fiction creatures with big eyes and tiny ears. No. Thank God, we shall be like Him.*

You will know me and I will recognize you.

Scripture makes it clear that there will be degrees of rewards in heaven based on what we did with the light that has been given to us. Everybody is going to be *somebody* in the Kingdom. And remember, you will reside in the City of God infinitely longer than you are here. In the words of *Amazing Grace:*

> *When we've been there ten thousand years,*
> *Bright shining as the sun,*
> *We've no less days to sing God's praise.*
> *Than when we first begun.*

A Life-Changing Prayer

Perhaps, as you've read this book, you have said to

yourself, "That is how I want to live. I wish I could know the peace he's talking about."

You can! And it begins with finding Christ.

Far more important than joining a church or embracing a religion is that you get right with God, through His Son, Jesus.

The Lord will hear your pleading and receive you unto Himself. Jesus said, "Him that cometh to me I will in no wise cast out" (John 6:37).

I want you to repeat with me the Sinner's Prayer. And if you say it sincerely, honestly and earnestly, He will do what you ask.

Will you stop for a moment and pray with me? Say these words out loud from your heart.

> *Oh, God,*
> *Be merciful to me, a sinner.*
> *Forgive me of my sin.*
> *Wash me in the blood of the Lord Jesus Christ.*
> *Save my soul and write my name in the Lamb's Book of Life*
> *I ask this in Jesus' name, and to His glory.*
> *Lord Jesus, by your Spirit come into my heart,*
> *And become Lord and Master of my life.*
> *From this day forward I'm yours to command.*
> *Thank you, Lord, for saving my soul.*

I believe you meant every word of that prayer.

FROM STRESS TO REST

Now make a commitment to study and meditate on God's Word every day, to pray and tell others of His great love.

I rejoice with you that you've taken the most important step on the path that leads to eternity — that leads *from stress to rest.*

Isaiah 43:2
Jeremiah 29:13

To Sue
To one of the best long-time friends I've ever had—

Remember God wishes you to prosper and be in health even as your soul prospers — 3 John 2

Read + meditate on daily

Psalm 103:1-5
Isaiah 53:4,5
1 Peter 2:24

Your healing has already been paid for... believe it & receive it. Remember also there is nothing too hard for God!

Love always,
Christine W—

9/98